YOU CAN'T
GET TO

HEAVEN

WITHOUT A

SPACE SUIT

THE
"SPIRITUALLY SCIENTIFIC" REASON WHY
YOU NEED JESUS

H.D. SHIVELY

ISBN 9780692474846

All scriptures are from the King James Version, adapted into modern English by the author

"And you shall know the truth, and the truth shall make you free"

John 8:32

CONTENTS

PART ONE

PART TWO

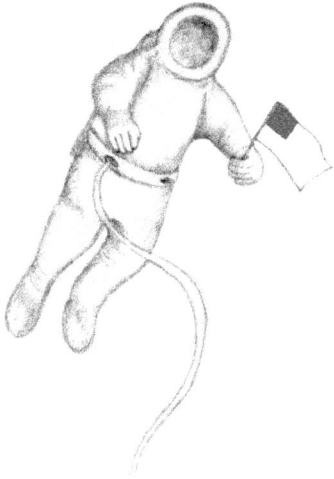

THIS LITTLE BOOK

IS DEDICATED

TO ALL THOSE WHO

ARE NOT AFRAID TO EXPLORE

THE UNIVERSE OF

GOD'S HOLY WORD

PART ONE

You can't get to Heaven

Without a Space Suit

Jesus said, *"I am the Way, the Truth and the Life; no one comes to the Father except by Me" (John 14:6).* Some respond to Jesus' absolute declaration by saying that it automatically condemns anyone who is of a different belief system; Buddhists, Hindus, Muslims, Jews, etc., are all excluded unless they are willing to come to God through the Messiah Jesus. But Jesus also said, *"God did not send His Son into the world to condemn the world, but that the world through Him might be saved" (John 3:17).*

Every human being on the planet, no matter what race, color, religion or creed, has one thing in common – we are all going to die someday. Human beings are already condemned to death in a universal pandemic, and the cause of this pandemic is sin. The Bible declares in Romans 3:23 that *"all have sinned and fall short of the glory of God."*

Sin is basically a rebellion against God's word, which can manifest in many ways, like lesions on a leper's skin. God has put the antidote to humanities' loathsome disease of sin in the blood of the Messiah Jesus. It is through faith in the death and resurrection of Jesus that this antidote is released to the believer.

A voice suddenly arises from the multitudes in the world who are opposing the Gospel message, and a representative emerges from the crowd and responds, "We know we have sinned. But God is a merciful God. He will let us into Heaven if we do our best and our good deeds outweigh the bad!"

To answer this one we must take a journey.

"Come with me my friend, and I will show you God's answer."

We suddenly find ourselves standing in the magnificent banqueting hall of Jesus' parable found in Matthew chapter twenty-two. Before us is a sumptuous feast ready to be enjoyed by a multitude of people all adorned in glowing white robes.

Jesus is there to greet you, my friend. He looks at you and He says, "Friend, how did you get in here without a wedding garment?"

You suddenly find that you are speechless. You thought you were dressed for the occasion. You very carefully picked out your own clothes and it took you many years to assemble an outfit that you thought would make you acceptable to God. You are shocked and horrified to hear Jesus, the King in this parable say to His servants, "Bind him hand and foot, and take him away, and cast him into outer darkness; there shall be weeping and gnashing of teeth. For many are called, but few are chosen."

You suddenly find yourself experiencing the horror of being rejected by the Lord and being subjected to the same

7

treatment God has reserved for demons; demons who know the will of God and reject it.

But because you are not dead yet, you still have a chance to repent and God wants you to understand. So, you find yourself standing with Adam and Eve after they had listened to the voice of deception that undermined God's commandment, by telling them that there would be no consequences for their disobedience (Genesis 3: 1-21).

They only had to disobey one commandment to sever their relationship with God, just one.

When they realized they were naked, they also fashioned an outfit of their own making using what materials were available, and we are told in the Genesis account that they covered themselves with leaves; leaves that would eventually dry up and wither away. The prophet Isaiah must have had this incident in mind when he said, *"But we are all as an unclean thing, and all our righteousnesses are as filthy rags; and we all do fade as a leaf; and our iniquities, like the wind, have taken us away"* (Isaiah 64:6).

Then we watch in amazement as an animal is slain and God clothes His shivering children with a work of His hands; and He adorns them with forgiveness in the warm skins of the first sacrifice (Genesis 3:21).

The point of it all is this – man cannot do what can only be done by an act of God. Man cannot make himself acceptable to God, he is incapable of ridding himself of his disease of sin. It must be done for him, by God, God's way according to the pattern and plan He has designed.

Now there is a "spiritually scientific" reason why the redemption of the human race must be accomplished precisely according to God's plan. In order to understand, we must make another journey through time which begins for us at the gates of fallen Eden.

We watch as God bans Adam and Eve from eating of the

8

tree of life because the fruit from that tree would give them and their offspring the ability to live forever on earth in their fallen state; showing us that human beings were never designed to live forever on earth apart from a provision from God. Yet they were designed in the image of God, which means their souls have eternal properties and will survive the death of the body. This is why we share the Gospel, to save souls from eternal separation from God and spiritual death.

Now this brings us to a vitally important point – human beings were never designed to inhabit Heaven – we were constructed to live forever in the earth realm in a state of perfection, a perfection that could only be maintained by obedience to God, and as we have seen, that obedience was not maintained and the world is enduring the consequences of Adam's original sin. If you don't believe in original sin, my friend, we all have an original sin lurking somewhere in our personal history, we all share Adam and Eve's corrupted DNA; we are all standing on the same feet of clay.

So what we have here is a world full of people that need to be rescued, "saved," so that their souls can be reunited with God after the death of the body and dwell with Him forever in His realm. In order for that to happen, our sin diseased souls need to be "converted," cleansed, and a provision must be made for souls that are designed to live on earth to be able to survive in Heaven's holy atmosphere, in the presence of a holy God.

Imagine an astronaut trying to survive in outer space without a space suit and the necessary oxygen it contains. He would die very quickly because he was not designed by His Creator to live in outer space.

Likewise, in order for our souls to survive in Heaven, we need to be equipped like that astronaut. The antidote for our sin and the equipment we need is provided for us through

God's wondrous plan of redemption.

This plan begins to unfold for us as we continue our journey through time in the pages of God's word.

We watch Adam and Eve's two sons bring their offerings to God. The Lord accepts Abel's gift from his flock, which is a symbol of the sacrifice that clothed their parents. But God rejects Cain's offering of the fruits of his labor from ground that God had cursed, and we are reminded again that we cannot please God apart from what He has chosen to make us acceptable to Him.

We proceed to the time of Abraham and we watch in suspense as he is about to sacrifice his beloved son. Then just at the moment when he is about to plunge in the knife, we sigh with relief as an angel intervenes and a ram is substituted for the offering. The boy's life is spared by a sacrifice provided by God.

Our journey continues and we enter Pharaoh's land at the moment when God's judgments against the Egyptian kingdom are coming to their conclusion.

God commands His people to put the blood of a sacrifice upon the doorposts of their houses and the plague of death upon the Egyptians firstborn would pass them by as God said in Exodus 12:13 - *"When I see the blood, I will pass over you, and the plague shall not be upon you to destroy you, when I smite the land of Egypt."*

The Israelites obeyed this command and their lives were spared by the blood of the Passover lamb.

Released from Pharaoh's bondage, we follow the Hebrew nation into the wilderness, a place of testing where God gives His laws through His servant Moses.

Now there are Ten Commandments that must be obeyed.

But before Moses even has the chance to present the word of God that had been written in stone, Moses finds to his dismay that his people are dancing around a golden calf, a god that their own hands had made, breaking the first commandment – *"you shall have no other gods before Me."* In response, Moses breaks the stones containing God's Word before the people showing them and us, that if you break one commandment, you have broken them all.

Moses returns to his mountain of intimacy with the Lord and he is given the commandments again, but this time he is also told to implement the plan and the pattern God had given Him for the construction of the tabernacle; the place where sacrifices would be made; sacrifices that would be accepted by God for the forgiveness of sins.

This is why the Apostle Paul said in Romans 5:14 that death reigned from Adam to Moses. Why did it stop at Moses? Because provision was made for the forgiveness of sins and the redemption of the people in the tabernacle sacrifices. Paul is telling us that no one can be saved without atonement.

God told Moses in Leviticus 17:11 - *"The life of the flesh is in the blood: and I have given it to you upon the altar to make an atonement for your souls: for it is the blood that makes an atonement for the soul."* God has never changed this requirement for the remission of sin. Never.

Does that mean that no one could be saved prior to the tabernacle sacrifices? Revelation thirteen, verse eight tells us that Jesus was *"slain from the foundation of the world."* God considered the atonement of Jesus a completed act even before its actual manifestation. We are shown from Jesus' parable of Lazarus and the rich man found in Luke sixteen that those who believed in God and died prior to the tabernacle sacrifices and Jesus' sacrifice, like Abraham, went to Paradise. Jesus' fulfillment of the atonement on Calvary released those souls from Paradise and enabled their entrance into Heaven and God's presence.

The instructions for atonement in the tabernacle services were to be followed precisely as God had given them to Moses with absolutely no deviations. When Aaron's sons decided to get creative and invented an offering of their own design, they were immediately fired, literally, and their charred corpses were carried from the tabernacle.

God dealt with them severely because unless God's pattern is followed precisely the result is death – for multitudes; because we cannot be outfitted for Heaven apart from what God has ordained. We can't "wing it" like Aaron's sons and deviate from the pattern. Man cannot add philosophy to God's formula and expect an altered version of God's plan of redemption to be accepted; and from a purely practical, spiritually scientific stand point – it just won't work.

Standing in the doorway of the tabernacle in this journey, we realize that everything we have been shown so far is a foreshadow or a type prefiguring the fulfillment of God's plan to rescue our souls from eternal spiritual death.

As we listen to the sounds of animals being slaughtered to make a temporary atonement for our sins, we look ahead to the fulfillment of the plan in Jesus, the prophesied Messiah, the Redeemer of mankind.

We continue on our journey toward a hill in the distance where the final once for all time sacrifice for our sins is to be made. We hear the prophet Isaiah's words accompanying us along the way. He speaks and his prophecy concerning the purpose of Messiah's coming flows around us like poetry.

He was wounded for our transgressions, bruised for our iniquities; the chastisement of our peace was upon Him, and with His stripes we are healed. All we like sheep have gone astray; we have turned every one to his own way; and the LORD has laid on Him the iniquity of us all. (Isaiah 53:5,6).

Yet it pleased the LORD to bruise Him; He has put Him to grief: when You shall make His soul an offering for sin (verse 10).

As the realization of this fact begins to take hold of our hearts, we suddenly find ourselves standing with the disciples at the foot of the cross where Jesus is being crucified.

We watch with the Apostle John as the centurion pierces Jesus' side with his spear, and we see the clear fluid from the heart's pericardial sac flow out with blood from the wound. Jesus' was clearly dead, for when that sac is pierced there can be no hope of resuscitation.

The Passover Lamb has been slain and placed in a tomb.

And here we wait for the prophesied moment to arrive, the new dawn when Jesus returns to life. And in this instant of resurrected victory we know that the plan that God has designed for the redemption of mankind has been victoriously completed.

We stand with the disciples before our resurrected Lord in awe and amazement.

Jesus' sacrifice has cleansed our believing souls and we have received His righteousness upon us. We are now clothed in our wedding garments, the "space suits" that make us acceptable and enables us to be invited into the universe of God's Holy Presence.

Now that we have been cleansed by faith in the atonement, we have been enabled to receive God's Holy Spirit. Then Jesus speaks to us as recorded in John 20:22, *"Receive the Holy Spirit!"* and He breathes into us His Eternal life giving Spirit that will enable our souls to live forever in Heaven's holy atmosphere.

If you still don't understand how all this works, we're going to get a bit technical here.

Jesus breathed the Holy Spirit into His disciples after His resurrection. The only other time that word "breathed" is used in the Scriptures is when God breathed the breath of life into Adam. In the Hebrew the word "breath" is "neshamah." The word in Hebrew for the Holy Spirit is "Ruach."

Therefore, Adam's life force was not the Ruach, the Holy Spirit. The "breath," the neshamah that animated Adam's body does not have the ability to enable the soul to breathe and live eternally in God's holy environment. Because humans were designed by God to live on earth, the neshamah was not designed to transport the soul into God's presence after the death of the body. The neshamah is not the oxygen of Heaven, it is designed only to give life to the human body on earth.

Jesus was given life as a man by the Ruach, the Holy Spirit as the scriptures record in Luke 1:35. The Holy Spirit came upon Mary, and God breathed His Spirit into her womb.

Paul notes the distinction between Adam and Jesus in first Corinthians 15:45 – *And so it is written, the first man Adam was made a living soul; the last Adam was made a quickening* (or life giving) *spirit.*

Jesus was made a life giving spirit.

Jesus said in John 5:26, *"As the Father has life in Himself, so He has given to the Son to have life in Himself."*

The life is in the blood as we have been shown in Leviticus 17:11, and that life in the blood of Jesus, is the Spirit of Eternal life, the Ruach, the Holy Spirit. And as Jesus has said in Matthew 10:20, the Holy Spirit is the Spirit of the Father. Jesus is the Son of God.

So you see this is why it is essential that we receive Jesus, and why we need Him; because it is only through faith in God's plan of redemption, the death and resurrection of the Messiah Jesus, that we can receive the Holy Spirit, and only the Holy Eternal Spirit of the living God gives us the ability to live eternally. It is the oxygen of Heaven and it has been placed by God in the blood of the Messiah to give to us through faith in His death and resurrection – God's plan for our redemption.

Jesus breathes that life in His blood, His Eternal Spirit, that oxygen we need to survive eternally in Heaven, into us when we believe.

14

We have reached the end of our journey and we now have learned the "Spiritually Scientific" reason why salvation can only be obtained through God's plan because the holy oxygen we need for our soul's survival in Heaven's holy atmosphere is only found in the blood of Jesus; the blood that is released to us by His sacrifice for our sins that makes us holy and gives us eternal life.

Before all of humanity there stands a great mountain. Its summit is hidden in the clouds of heaven. Each one of us is making a journey up that mountain seeking to obtain the summit where God and eternity resides.

No matter what our religion, we are all one in this endeavor, but as we continue upward, we find that the air is getting thinner, rarer. We discover to our dismay that we cannot continue to the summit for the air in that realm is too rare and holy for us to breathe.

Then out from humanities' multitudes that have been forced to remain behind, emerges a remnant clothed in white, marching upward in triumph and gratitude. These ones continue on to the summit and disappear into the holy mist of God's abode because they have been equipped for the journey by faith and they can breathe the rare air of Heaven.

Will you be among those who are clothed in the garments that only God can provide through faith in the death and resurrection of the Lord Jesus?

If you don't as yet have your space suit and the oxygen you need to survive in Heaven, it's easy to obtain. Believe that Jesus died for your sins and rose from the dead as the Scriptures proclaim. Then repent. Admit you have sinned and you need His forgiveness. Ask Him to forgive your sins, then invite Him into your heart to be the Lord of your life. It's as easy as praying and He will give you all the equipment you need for your adventure with Him in eternity.

In this journey we have watched Jesus die on a cross for our sins. We stood before His empty tomb and beheld Him breathing His eternal life giving Spirit into His disciples' souls. If you believe – Jesus is standing before you now and He is asking you to do one thing – "Inhale!"

HE BREATHED ON THEM,

AND SAID TO THEM,

"RECEIVE THE HOLY SPIRIT."

JOHN 20:22

THE PRINCIPLES OF SALVATION

Before His crucifixion, Jesus told His disciples that He would be going to prepare a place for them and that He would come again so that they would be with Him. Jesus used references to Hebrew marriage customs several times in His teachings and this is one of them.–

In my Father's house are many mansions: if it were not so, I would have told you. I go to prepare a place for you.

And if I go and prepare a place for you, I will come again, and receive you unto myself; that where I am, there you may be also (John 14:2,3).

In His parable of the ten virgins (Matthew 25:1-13), Jesus is the Bridegroom who returns to collect His waiting bride.

When a Hebrew couple was to be married, they first participated in an engagement ceremony. They began by separately taking a bath called a mikveh. Christians liken this custom to baptism.

The betrothal/engagement was so binding that the only way it could be broken was if either the bride or the groom were found to be unfaithful, then a divorce would have to be obtained, even though the couple had not as yet been formally married.

After the betrothal ceremony, the bridegroom left to build a house for his bride. The process usually took about a year. In the meantime the bride would prepare herself for the wedding. Then when the bride's new home was finally completed, the bridegroom would come for her unexpectedly, so she always needed to be in a state of readiness.

Relating this back to John 14:2,3; Jesus is the bridegroom who was going away to prepare a home for his bride, His church.

The Hebrew wedding tradition is also a similitude of the principles of salvation that God has instigated through the Bridegroom, the Messiah Jesus. Through faith in God's plan of redemption, Jesus' atoning death and His resurrection from the dead, we are betrothed to our Bridegroom. We have been baptized as an evidence of our commitment. We are saved at this point under a contract that is so binding that the only way it can be broken is by our unfaithfulness. If we deny our Bridegroom, He will deny us (Matthew 10:33).

There are three stages associated with salvation that relate to the Hebrew marriage tradition, which was also recognized by the apostles.

But we had the sentence of death in ourselves, that we should not trust in ourselves, but in God who raises the dead; who delivered us from so great a death, and does deliver: in whom we trust that He will yet deliver us (II Corinthians 1:9, 10 KJV).

We are saved, we are being saved, and we will be saved when we are retrieved by our Bridegroom, and we receive "the outcome of our faith," the salvation of our souls (I Peter 1:9). In the meantime during our betrothal period we are being "kept by the power of God through faith unto salvation ready to be revealed at the last time" (I Peter 1:5). The "last time" is a reference to the end when our souls are released from our bodies and our bridegroom has come for us.

We are saved. We have been betrothed to Jesus by faith. Again nothing can break this union except our own unfaithfulness and disobedience to His commandment to forgive others (Matthew 6:14,15). If we do not forgive, then our heavenly Father will not forgive us and we cannot be formally married, so to speak.

We are being saved. During the engagement period before the Lord returns to gather us into His embrace, we prepare ourselves for our appearance at the judgment seat of Christ where we will give an account of what we have allowed the

Holy Spirit to accomplish in us toward the goal of becoming like our Bridegroom (II Corinthians 5:10). The evidence of our development into Christ-likeness is revealed in how we have treated others in our lifetimes on earth (Matthew 25:31-46). This judgment is for rewards for true believers and not condemnation.

We will be saved. The third stage is when we receive the outcome of our faith, the salvation of our souls "Receiving the end of your faith, even the salvation of your souls" (I Peter 1:9). We have remained faithful during our engagement period, and are figuratively formally "married" when our souls have reached their final destination with our Bridegroom.

So we can prepare for our bridegroom knowing that we are saved in a betrothal that is as binding as the actual marriage. As long as we remain faithful to our Husband and remain in the faith, we can anticipate with joy, the moment when we hear the angels announce that our Bridegroom is coming.

Your Bridegroom could come for you at any time. Are you ready for that moment? Are you adjusting your spiritual appearance in the looking glass of His words? Do you see the reflection of His character in your own? The degree of love we feel for our Bridegroom, affects the zeal with which we attend to our spiritual development, so we will not be ashamed before Him at His coming (I John 2:28). Read His words, commune with Him in daily prayer. Ask Him for the things you need; the fruits of His Spirit that are so pleasing to Him (Galatians 5:22,23) and He will be faithful in adorning you with those spiritual jewels of His love. What a beautiful bride you will be!

THE FAITH OF ABRAHAM
AND THE GRACE THAT WORKS

Bible genealogies may be boring to read for some, but they are important. They provide the link between the first man Adam, and the last Adam, Jesus the Messiah.

God preserved Noah and his family from being wiped out in the great flood; of Noah's three sons, Japheth, Ham and Shem, Shem's linage was chosen to be the family line that would produce the Messiah. Shem's linage is singled out and detailed in Genesis 11. Shem's descendant, Abraham, was designated by God to be the Father of Israel, and is first mentioned in verse 26 of that chapter.

Chapter 12 begins his story and we are going to focus on his relationship with God and how it relates to the Messiah and the Christian faith.

Abraham had settled with his family in Haran (Genesis 11:31). When Abraham was 75 years old, God spoke to him and told him to leave everything he had known and go to a land God would show him. Let's read verses one through four of Genesis chapter 12.

Gen 12:1 Now the LORD had said to Abram, "You get out of your country, and from your kindred, and from your father's house, to a land that I will show you:
Gen 12:2 And I will make of you a great nation, and I will bless you, and make your name great; and you shall be a blessing:
Gen 12:3 And I will bless them that bless you, and curse him that curses you: and in you shall all families of the earth be blessed."

Gen 12:4 So Abram departed, as the LORD had spoken to him; and Lot went with him: and Abram was seventy and five years old when he departed out of Haran.

It's important to understand that Abraham had a very close relationship with God that enabled him to be led directly by God's voice, His Spirit. In this, Abraham is an example of the Christian who has believed the Gospel, and received the Holy Spirit through faith in Jesus' death and resurrection from the dead. This enables a sincere believer to be led by the Holy Spirit like Abraham. Abraham's faith is a foreshadow of the faith of believers in the Messiah Jesus.

Under the Old Covenant, only a select few were permitted to experience the Holy Spirit like Abraham, David and the prophets. In the New Covenant, all who receive Jesus as their Messiah and believe the gospel are given this privilege.

Abraham believed God when he was told to leave his home and all that was familiar to him. Because Abraham's faith was genuine, he obeyed God, which was his first step in an historic journey that would result in many blessings.

Abraham was childless, yet God told him that he would have a child in his old age with his equally old wife Sarah, a medical impossibility. Yet we read in Genesis 15, verse 6: –

"And he believed in the LORD, and He counted it to him for righteousness."

Abraham's faith is used as an example of the Christian faith in the New Testament. Let's read what the Apostle Paul says in Romans chapter 4, verses 1 through 8.

Rom 4:1 What shall we say then that Abraham our father, as pertaining to the flesh, has found?
Rom 4:2 For if Abraham were justified by works, he has something to boast about; but not before God.
Rom 4:3 For what says the scripture? Abraham believed God,

and it was counted to him for righteousness.

Rom 4:4 Now to him who works, the wages are not counted as grace but as debt.

Rom 4:5 But to him that does not work, but believes on him that justifies the ungodly, his faith is counted for righteousness.

Rom 4:6 Even as David also described the blessedness of the man, to whom God imputes righteousness without works,

Rom 4:7 Saying, Blessed are they whose iniquities are forgiven, and whose sins are covered.

Rom 4:8 Blessed is the man to whom the Lord will not impute sin.

The Apostle Paul has recognized that God justified Abraham by Abraham's faith apart from any works. Likewise, Christians are justified by faith in Jesus' atonement. Justification is by God's grace alone and cannot be obtained through any self-effort. It is a gift, as Jesus said in John 3:16 "For God so loved the world, that He gave His only begotten Son, that whoever believes in Him, should not perish, but have everlasting life."

Our salvation is a gift based on faith in Jesus' atoning sacrifice for our sins, and it is not something that can be earned because as the Apostle Paul writes in Romans 3:23, - For all have sinned and fall short of the glory of God.

Paul is merely reiterating a principle of scripture that he quotes in the previous verse 10, which is taken from Psalm 14, "As it is written, 'There is none righteous, no not one.'" That is, no one can be righteous enough to justify themselves before a holy God, it must be by faith alone.

Here we can return to Genesis chapter three. After Adam and Eve sinned they tried to cover themselves with leaves, or their own efforts. God made them coats of skins from the first death recorded in Genesis. They had to be covered by a sacrifice made by God Himself, which is the foreshadow of God's plan of redemption. Our sins can only be covered by an act of God, which was Jesus' sacrifice for our sins. Let's read Galatians three, verses 5 through 14.

Gal 3:5 He therefore that ministers to you the Spirit, and works miracles among you, does he do it by the works of the law, or by the hearing of faith?
Gal 3:6 Even as Abraham believed God, and it was accounted to him for righteousness.
Gal 3:7 you know therefore that they which are of faith, the same are the children of Abraham.
Gal 3:8 And the scripture, foreseeing that God would justify the heathen through faith, preached before the gospel to Abraham, saying, In you shall all nations be blessed.
Gal 3:9 So then they which be of faith are blessed with faithful Abraham.
Gal 3:10 For as many as are of the works of the law are under the curse: for it is written, Cursed is every one that continues not in all things which are written in the book of the law to do them.
Gal 3:11 But that no man is justified by the law in the sight of God, it is evident: for, The just shall live by faith.
Gal 3:12 And the law is not of faith: but, The man that does them shall live in them.
Gal 3:13 Christ has redeemed us from the curse of the law, being made a curse for us: for it is written, Cursed is every one that hangs on a tree:
Gal 3:14 That the blessing of Abraham might come on the Gentiles through Jesus Christ; that we might receive the promise of the Spirit through faith.

In other words, we can't point to our own efforts to justify ourselves before God. That's like covering ourselves in fig leaves. We can only be justified by faith in God's plan of redemption that He instigated in Eden.

Here are three other examples from scripture to illustrate this principle.

Matthew's gospel describes an encounter with Jesus and a rich young man in chapter 19 verses 16 through 22. The young man came up to Jesus and asked, "Good Master, what shall I do to inherit eternal life?"

"Why do you call Me good?" Jesus answered as the God-Man assessed the situation. "There is none good except God alone."

In other words, how "good" do you think you can be?

Undaunted, the young man kept staring at Him earnestly, so Jesus continued. "You know the commandments…"

"I have kept all of them all my life," the young man answered.

Then Jesus said, "One thing you lack, sell all you have, give it to the poor, then come and follow Me."

Suddenly disqualified, the rich young man turned away leaving the first commandment, "You shall have no other gods before Me" shattered in his wake. He was putting his stuff before God. He was actually an idolater and didn't know it.

Jesus sighed as He watched the young man wander sadly back to his possessions. Then the Lord turned and walked determinedly toward the Cross in the distance to purchase an entrance into heaven for all those who could never be "good" enough. "For with God all things are possible." - Mark 10:23

In Luke's gospel chapter 18 verses 9-14, Jesus gives us a parable about two people praying to God. One is a Pharisee, an accomplished religious leader who is comparing himself to the sinner who is also praying. The Pharisee says, "God, I thank You, that I am not as other men are, extortioners, unjust, adulterers, or even as this publican. I fast twice in the week, I give tithes of all that I possess."

And the tax collector, standing afar off, would not lift up so much as his eyes to heaven, but smote upon his breast, saying, "God be merciful to me a sinner."

Jesus says, "I tell you, this man went down to his house justified rather than the other: for every one that exalts himself shall be abased; and he that humbles himself shall be exalted."

The Apostle Peter reiterates, in I Peter 5:5 – "God resists the proud and gives grace to the humble."

And finally we are given this example at Jesus' crucifixion In Luke's Gospel chapter 23, verses 39-43. Jesus was crucified between two criminals.

Luke 23: 39 And one of the criminals which were hanged railed on Him, saying, "If you are the Messiah, save yourself and us."

Luke 23:40 But the other answering rebuked him, saying, "You do not fear God, seeing you are in the same condemnation?

Luke 23:41 And we indeed justly; for we receive the due reward of our deeds: but this man has done nothing wrong."

Luke 23:42 And he said to Jesus, "Lord, remember me when you come into Your kingdom."

Luke 23:43 And Jesus said to him, "Truly I say to you, today you shall be with Me in paradise."

All that repentant man had to do to inherit eternal life was to believe that Jesus was the Messiah, the fulfillment of God's plan of redemption. He was accepted even though he did not have the time or opportunity to do any work for God.

However we can see from the examples in Abraham's life, that his faith produced obedience to do what God's Spirit was telling him to do. When God told Abraham to sacrifice his miracle child, Isaac, the promised son of his old age,

Abraham was willing and was about to plunge a knife into his son when an angel intervened at the last moment, sparing the boy. God provided a ram for the sacrifice in Isaac's place. This account is recorded in Genesis 22.

The Apostle James recognized this relationship between a genuine faith and obedience. He writes about it in chapter 2, verses 17 through 24 in his epistle. Let's read it for ourselves.

Jas 2:17 Even so faith, if it has not works, is dead, being alone.
Jas 2:18 Yes, a man may say, You have faith, and I have works: show me your faith without your works, and I will show you my faith by my works.
Jas 2:19 You believe that there is one God; you do well: the devils also believe, and tremble.
Jas 2:20 But will you know, O vain man, that faith without works is dead?
Jas 2:21 Was not Abraham our father justified by works, when he had offered Isaac his son upon the altar?
Jas 2:22 You see how faith worked with his works, and by works was faith made perfect?
Jas 2:23 And the scripture was fulfilled which says, Abraham believed God, and it was imputed to him for righteousness: and he was called the Friend of God.
Jas 2:24 You see then how that by works a man is justified, and not by faith only.

Let's look at verse 22 again. – You see how faith worked with his works, and by works was faith made perfect – or I would say perfected or complete. The natural produce or fruit of a genuine living faith will produce obedience, just like it did for Abraham. But works by itself without faith in God's plan of redemption cannot justify anyone. Obedience is the evidence that a faith is genuine or sincere. We really cannot have one without the other, they operate hand in hand.

We have to look at Jesus' words in John 15. He is the vine, God is the husbandman who operates by His Holy Spirit through His Son through us. It is the sap of the Holy Spirit operating in our lives that produces the fruit or holy character that is pleasing to God. Let's read John 15, verses 1-6.

John: 1 I am the true vine, and my Father is the husbandman.
John 15:2 Every branch in me that bears not fruit he takes away: and every branch that bears fruit, he purges it, that it may bring forth more fruit.
John 15:3 Now you are clean through the word which I have spoken to you.
John 15:4 Abide in me, and I in you. As the branch cannot bear fruit of itself, except it abide in the vine; no more can you, except you abide in me.
John 15:5 I am the vine, you are the branches: He that abides in me, and I in him, the same brings forth much fruit: for without me you can do nothing.
John 15:6 If a man abides not in me, he is cast forth as a branch, and is withered; and men gather them, and cast them into the fire, and they are burned.

It is obvious here that we can do nothing without Jesus. "For without Me you can do nothing." In other words, no work that we do apart from faith in Jesus will justify us. It is the work that is produced naturally though our union with God through Jesus that justifies us, or is the evidence of our faith in the atonement as the Apostle James understood. "Faith without works is a dead faith." A dead faith is a faith that is not abiding in the vine of Christ.

Let's take a look at the Apostle Paul's words in Ephesians chapter 2 verse 2 through 10.

Eph 2:2 Wherein in time past you walked according to the

course of this world, according to the prince of the power of the air, the spirit that now works in the children of disobedience:

Eph 2:3 Among whom also we all had our conversation in times past in the lusts of our flesh, fulfilling the desires of the flesh and of the mind; and were by nature the children of wrath, even as others.

Eph 2:4 But God, who is rich in mercy, for his great love wherewith he loved us,

Eph 2:5 Even when we were dead in sins, has quickened us together with Christ, (by grace you are saved;)

Eph 2:6 And has raised us up together, and made us sit together in heavenly places in Christ Jesus:

Eph 2:7 That in the ages to come he might show the exceeding riches of his grace in his kindness toward us through Christ Jesus.

Eph 2:8 For by grace you are saved through faith; and that not of yourselves: it is the gift of God: Eph 2:9 Not of works, lest any man should boast.

Eph 2:10 For we are his workmanship, created in Christ Jesus to good works, which God has before ordained that we should walk in them.

It is God who does His work through us. And the works that He produces through us are the works that He accepts to be rewarded.

Every believer needs to understand that when we die we all must stand before the judgment seat of Christ. Paul says in Romans 14:10 - But why do you judge your brother? Or why do you show contempt for your brother? For we shall all stand before the judgment seat of Christ.

After the death of the body and the soul is released, when Jesus returns, every believer must stand before Jesus at His judgment seat to receive a reward for the things that were done in his body, good and bad. A true believer is not condemned because of his saving faith in Jesus' atonement for his sins, but he will be chastened and/or rewarded for his works: his response to the gospel.

This is something that we must keep in mind during our daily walk with the Lord. We repent of our sins when we receive Jesus, and whenever the Holy Spirit convicts us of sin, we need to acknowledge those things and repent of them as well. This repentance is not for salvation which we have already received and is a done deal; this repentance is for our rewards, and spiritual growth, and maturity into the image of Jesus' character, which is the goal of the Christian life.
Let's read in I Corinthians chapter three, verses 11-15 to see what the Apostle Paul has to say about what happens at Jesus' judgment seat.

1Co 3:11 For other foundation can no man lay than that is laid, which is Jesus Christ.
1Co 3:12 Now if any man build upon this foundation gold, silver, precious stones, wood, hay, stubble;
1Co 3:13 Every man's work shall be made manifest: for the day shall declare it, because it shall be revealed by fire; and the fire shall try every man's work of what sort it is.
1Co 3:14 If any man's work abides which he has built thereupon, he shall receive a reward.
1Co 3:15 If any man's work shall be burned, he shall suffer loss: but he himself shall be saved; yet so as by fire.

The foundation is the gospel, Jesus' sacrifice and resurrection. He alone is the foreordained Messiah who can save us. How we live in response to the gospel will be rewarded or burned at the judgment. All true believers want to let God have His way in their lives and are willing to let

Him change them into the people He wants them to be. The Holy Spirit, which is Jesus' and the Father's Spirit, helps us to walk in the good works that He has ordained for us. Those good works are illustrated for us in the law He gave to Moses which is exemplified and illustrated for us in Jesus' example.

We read God's word so that we can learn about the things He likes and doesn't like, so we can choose to do the things that please Him. When we sin deliberately after knowledge, we can open the door to demonic attacks, which God will use to drive us back into His will for our lives. We can look at His word as a bunch of laws to follow, or we can see it as a book of wisdom that is designed to be a guide for our health and spiritual welfare.

It's also important to understand that many of the ordinances recorded in the Old Testament were for the Jews specifically at that time to keep them separate from the pagan practices of the cultures around them. But the moral law always remains which is made very clear by Jesus and His Apostles.

Abraham was also given the law orally before it was written down by Moses 430 years later. God says to Abraham in Genesis 18 verse 19, - "For I know him, that he will command his children and his household after him, and they shall keep the way of the LORD, to do justice and judgment; that the LORD may bring upon Abraham that which He has spoken of him."

Obedience produces blessings. As we keep God's word and allow ourselves to be led by His Spirit, He keeps His promises to bless us, and there is no greater blessing to a soul that is seeking God, than to be blessed by His presence in our daily lives and have that relationship with God that Abraham experienced.

Abraham was called the friend of God. What a wonderful thing it is to be the close personal friend of the great God who created the universe and everything it contains.

Faith in God's plan of redemption in Jesus enables us to have that relationship. Because of Abraham's faith and obedience, God fulfilled His promise to him and Abraham indeed became the father of many nations.

So we've learned from Romans 3:28, that "a man is justified by faith without the deeds of the law." And that a genuine faith will result in obedience to God's word, which is an evidence of his faith. That is the sense in which we are justified by works.

I want to conclude by reading the Apostle Paul's exhortation to us in Romans chapter six.

Rom 6:1 What shall we say then? Shall we continue in sin, that grace may abound?

Rom 6:2 God forbid. How shall we, that are dead to sin, live any longer in it?

Rom 6:3 Don't you know, that so many of us as were baptized into Jesus Christ were baptized into his death?

Rom 6:4 Therefore we are buried with him by baptism into death: that like as Christ was raised up from the dead by the glory of the Father, even so we also should walk in newness of life.

Rom 6:5 For if we have been planted together in the likeness of his death, we shall be also in the likeness of his resurrection:

Rom 6:6 Knowing this, that our old man is crucified with him, that the body of sin might be destroyed, that from now on we should not serve sin.

Rom 6:7 For he that is dead is freed from sin.

Rom 6:8 Now if we are dead with Christ, we believe that we shall also live with him:

Rom 6:9 Knowing that Christ being raised from the dead dies no more; death has no more dominion over him.

Rom 6:10 For in that he died, he died to sin once: but in that he lives, he lives to God.

Rom 6:11 Likewise you also reckon yourselves to be dead indeed to sin, but alive to God through Jesus Christ our Lord.

Rom 6:12 Let not sin therefore reign in your mortal body, that you should obey it in its lusts. Rom 6:13 Neither yield your members as instruments of unrighteousness to sin: but yield yourselves to God, as those that are alive from the dead, and your members as instruments of righteousness to God.

Rom 6:14 For sin shall not have dominion over you: for you are not under the law, but under grace.

Rom 6:15 What then? shall we sin, because we are not under the law, but under grace? God forbid.

Rom 6:16 Don't you know, that to whom you yield yourselves servants to obey, his servants you are to whom you obey; whether of sin to death, or of obedience to righteousness?

Rom 6:17 But God be thanked, that you were the servants of sin, but you have obeyed from the heart that form of doctrine which was delivered you.

Rom 6:18 Being then made free from sin, you became the servants of righteousness.

Rom 6:19 I speak after the manner of men because of the infirmity of your flesh: for as you have yielded your members servants to uncleanness and to iniquity to iniquity; even so now yield your members servants to righteousness to holiness.

Rom 6:20 For when you were the servants of sin, you were free from righteousness.

Rom 6:21 What fruit had you then in those things whereof you are now ashamed? for the end of those things is death.

Rom 6:22 But now being made free from sin, and become servants to God, you have your fruit to holiness, and the end everlasting life.

Rom 6:23 For the wages of sin is death; but the gift of God is eternal life through Jesus Christ our Lord.

I want to go back a little bit to James' statement, even "the devils believe and they tremble." What makes the difference between a believing devil and a believing Christian? They both believe that Jesus is the Son of God and that He rose from the dead and is the Messiah. The difference is your relationship with God and your walk with God and your love for God. Devils can't worship God, they can't follow God, they can't repent of their sin, but you can. You can make the difference between a believing devil and a true, repentant believing Christian.

MANASSEH'S STORY OF REPENTANCE

"It's too late for me," he said. "I've done too many bad things for the Lord to forgive me."

This statement arose from a man we were ministering to at one of our outreaches. We tried to convince him that when we repent, and receive Jesus by faith in His atoning death and His resurrection from the dead, our sins are removed and He gives us the gift of eternal life and a brand new beginning. No one is ever beyond His mercy when we recognize that we have sinned and we need Him.

I hoped and prayed that our ministry to this man that day changed his heart and his mind. He took our words and wandered away in silence.

I believe this man is a representative of many who are imprisoned with the same view.

If you are one of those individuals who feels that you are beyond the reach of God's forgiving grace, I want to share with you an example from the Scriptures of God's willingness to forgive even the vilest of sinners.

This example is taken from II Chronicles, chapter thirty-three, verses one through nineteen.

The Scriptures paint a picture for us of one of the most evil kings in the Bible's record of the history of God's people. Manasseh was appointed king of Israel when he was twelve years old. Manasseh's father was the good king Hezekiah, but his son did not follow his dad's example. The list of Manasseh's crimes is extensive. God had cast out the evil influences of the pagan nations surrounding Israel, but Manasseh embraced the abominations that the Lord condemned, and brought that wickedness back into Israel's camp with zealous delight.

We are told that he rebuilt all the pagan altars that His father had destroyed, (II Chronicles 33:3). He defiled the LORD's sanctuary with altars to "the hosts of heaven," demon entities, (verses 4, 5). He restored the worship of Baalim, which incorporated fornication and perverted sexual sin as part of its rituals along with the sacrifice of children. He practiced witchcraft, consorting with familiar spirits and wizards (male witches), which is strictly forbidden by God, and warranted the death penalty according to Moses.

The perversion and idolatry he caused Israel to practice, brought the whole nation into sin – "worse than the heathen whom the LORD had destroyed before the children of Israel" (verse 9).

When archeologists were examining the remains of these civilizations that God had eliminated, the consensus among those experts was not, "Why did God destroy them?" but, "Why did He wait so long?" The practices the archeologists discovered were so vile, they marveled at God's allowing them to continue for so long. This again is evidence of God's unwillingness that any should perish and His mercy is even extended to those who are extremely wicked – for a season.

We are told that Manasseh's sins were worse than those pagan nations, which makes it hard to fathom the depths of degradation that had been permitted to reign within God's holy Jerusalem.

God in His mercy, sent His prophets to try and bring His people to repentance, but they refused to listen (verse 33). Consistent with the Biblical pattern, Manasseh's sins opened the door for Divine chastisement. God withdrew His protection and God allowed Israel's enemies to consume them and they were attacked by the King of Assyria.

Manasseh was taken captive, and it was in the darkness of

his God ordained captivity, that the evil heart of king Manasseh was genuinely broken.

God knows what it takes to bring the straying ones back into His embrace. We are shown that when Manasseh "was in affliction, he besought the LORD his God, and humbled himself greatly before the God of his fathers, and prayed to Him: and He was entreated of him, and heard his supplications…" (verses 12,13).

God saw that Manasseh's prayers of repentance were sincere and genuine. Biblical repentance requires a willingness to turn from sin. Motivated by a healthy fear of God, the man who was bound by the chains of his own wrong doing, was miraculously set free and restored.

The Scriptures do not give us the details of Manasseh's release and the reasons why the victorious Assyrian king decided to release his prisoner and restore Israel. God may have used some of the techniques he orchestrated upon Pharaoh, or He may have demanded Israel's restoration in terrifying night visions to the Assyrian king. Whatever means the LORD used to accomplish His goals were viewed as miraculous to Manasseh and the final result was he knew at last that the God of Israel is the true God and deserving of all worship and devotion (verse 13).

Motivated by God's act of forgiveness and mercy, and a miraculous deliverance coupled with a renewed reverent fear of God, Manasseh reversed his behavior, removed all the remnants of his idolatry from God's house and restored the people back to pure worship.

Manasseh died restored and totally forgiven, in spite of the depravity of his sin.

The point of Manasseh's story of repentance is this – if God can forgive an evil dude like Manasseh, He is more than willing to forgive you; if you, like Manasseh, are willing to repent and let God break the chain of your bondage and give you a new beginning.

Jesus' sacrifice for our sins was ordained from the foundation of the world (Revelation 13:8) and it is upon the merits of that perfect sacrifice that forgiveness was meted upon Manasseh then, and for us today.

God is reaching out to you with His arms of mercy in His Son, Jesus, who is the Image (Colossian 1:15), of the God who loves you. There is no sin so vile that it cannot be removed and forgiven when it is acknowledged and confessed at the feet of our risen Savior.

The apostle John assures us that "If we confess our sins, He is faithful and just to forgive us our sins, and to cleanse us from all unrighteousness" – just like Manasseh. (I John 1:9).

THE FATHER'S HEART

As a father has compassion on his children, so the LORD has compassion on them that fear Him. - Psalm 103:13

I was explaining the Gospel to a young woman who had not as yet made a commitment to Jesus. The one stumbling block that was preventing her from accepting the Gospel was as she said, "I can't understand how someone who has done horrible things like murder, rape and child molestation can receive God's forgiveness."

I answered, "If you had a child that did those things and he came to you genuinely repentant and begged for your forgiveness, would you forgive him?"

She replied in an instant, "Well, yes, I would forgive him because he was my child."

I smiled. "Do you see? It is the same way with God. He is our loving Father and He will always forgive any sin, no matter how vile, if there is genuine repentance, because He loves us and sees all those who are willing to come to Him through the Messiah Jesus as His children."

She understood immediately and the barrier that had prevented her from receiving Jesus as her Savior was removed.

God looks at the heart and many of us that see ourselves as "righteous" are sometimes actually just as vile in our thought lives as those we deem as gross sinners. We need to remember that the tenth commandment, "Thou shalt not covet" was meant to explore those inner motives that would disqualify us from entrance to Heaven and God's holy presence.

The Word of God tells us in Romans 3:23 that, "all have sinned, and come short of the glory of God." All of us must come to God humbly, willing to repent of our sins and be forgiven through the love He has exemplified for us though the sacrifice of the Messiah Jesus for our sins.

PART TWO

Why Jesus
has to be the Messiah

ISAIAH 40:12
AND
PROVERBS 30:4

Who has
Measured the waters
in the hollow of His hand,
And meted out heaven with the span,
And comprehended the dust of the earth in a measure,
And weighed the mountains in scales,
And the hills in a balance?

Who has
Ascended up into heaven, or descended?
Who has gathered the wind in His fists?
Who has bound the waters in a garment?
Who has established all the ends of the earth?
What is His name,

And what is
His Son's name,
If you can tell?

WHY JESUS HAS TO BE
THE MESSIAH

While the Israelites were still enduring their captivity in Babylon, the prophet Daniel, who like other prophets had received visions from the Lord of future events, was now visited by an angel who showed him the future concerning the Messiah and the second temple. This prophecy is called, "The Prophecy of the Seventy Weeks." This prophecy is also about the redemption from sin.

Seventy weeks are determined upon your people and your holy city, to finish the transgression, and to make an end of sins, and to make reconciliation for iniquity, and to bring in everlasting righteousness, and to seal up the vision and prophecy, and to anoint the most holy (Daniel 9:24).

God's plan of redemption for the human race was foreshadowed in Eden when He made a sacrifice to cover His naked children, (Genesis 3:21) and cumulates with the arrival of the prophesied Messiah. Thus that vision is to be "sealed up," finished or concluded when the Messiah makes "reconciliation for iniquity" (Daniel 9:24).

In this chapter we are shown that Daniel had been reading the prophet Jeremiah and he discovered that Jeremiah had foretold that the captivity would last seventy years. We can imagine Daniel's exhilaration when he realized that their seventy year sentence had reached its conclusion. This knowledge propelled Daniel into a heartfelt and earnest prayer of repentance for his sins and the sins of his people. In response to that prayer, Daniel was visited by an angel who revealed the secrets of the future to this one who was to God "greatly beloved."

Daniel is told that Jerusalem, which had been destroyed would be rebuilt along with the temple. The city would be destroyed again, but before that the Messiah, the Anointed One would be killed, "cut off." (Daniel 9:26).

Know therefore and understand, that from the going forth of the commandment to restore and to build Jerusalem unto the Messiah the Prince shall be seven weeks, and threescore and two weeks: the street shall be built again, and the wall, in troublous times (verse 25).

We have already been shown that this prophecy was fulfilled. The Jews were permitted to return to Jerusalem and build the second temple.

And after threescore and two weeks shall Messiah be cut off, but not for Himself:.... (Some Hebrew translations read 'and will be no more').

The Messiah would be killed and then: -

... and the people of the prince that shall come shall destroy the city and the sanctuary; and the end shall be with a flood, and unto the end of the war desolations are determined (verse 26).

So far we have been shown that Jerusalem would be rebuilt, then the Messiah would come after the, "*seven weeks, and threescore and two weeks,*" be killed, and the city will be destroyed once again. The prophet Daniel has clearly been shown that the promised Messiah would come before the destruction of Jerusalem and the second temple. The prophecy of the destruction of the second temple was fulfilled in 70AD, forty years after Jesus also prophesied of its destruction because "they did not know the time of their visitation;" they did not recognize that Messiah had come (Luke 19:44).

In chapter three of Malachi's prophecy, God says through the prophet, *"Behold, I will send My messenger, and he shall prepare the way before Me: and the <u>Lord</u>, whom you seek, shall suddenly come to His temple, even the <u>messenger</u> of the covenant, whom you delight in: behold, He shall come, says the LORD (YHWH) of hosts" (Malachi 3:1).*

When the prophecy of Malachi was given, the Jews had been allowed to return to their land and the temple had been rebuilt. The prophecy states that the Lord will come to His temple and He is the messenger of the covenant. "He shall come, says the LORD of hosts." That's God talking about the Messiah, the Lord, coming to the temple. It would have been the understanding of the people at that time that Messiah was coming to that new temple, which He did before it was destroyed, according to Daniel 9:25,26.

The first part of the verse is referring to John the Baptist the messenger/prophet who would prepare the way before the Lord, who is the messenger of the covenant. That covenant would be the prophesied New Everlasting Covenant (Jeremiah 32:40, Isaiah 55:3).

The wording used here in the Hebrew for Lord can also be used to designate God, but in the scriptures God is not referred to as a messenger, that term is reserved for prophets. So here we have a prophet designated by the word messenger, who can also be referred to as God, according to the usage of the word in Hebrew, being sent by God (YHWH). No one fulfills the description better than Jesus, the Messiah.

There are some who claim that Daniel's verses 25 and 26 are referring to two "anointed ones" because of the wording in some Hebrew translations. –

...until the time of an anointed prince (verse 25).

44

...an anointed one shall be cut off (verse 26).

The word "anointed" is pronounced as "messiah" in these scriptures and is used for both. While the word "anointed" is used in association with many individuals in the scriptures, there is only one prophesied messiah that is to be the long awaited redeemer of Israel. That redeemer is to be a "priest after the order of Melchisedec" (Psalm 110:4), who was a king and also a priest.

In Daniel 9:25 and 26, we see these same two characteristics associated with one "Messiah." He is a prince and an anointed one, a description that is also used for priests.

Daniel's prophecy has been perfectly fulfilled. Even if the Jews did not recognize Jesus as the messiah at that time, they still acknowledged that He did miracles. The Jewish historian Josephus also recorded that Jesus did miracles, which certainly would qualify Him as being anointed. So we see in Daniel's prophecy the anointed one killed before the destruction of the city, and the "prince that is to come" emerges from the people who destroyed the city in 70 AD (verse 26).

We have to understand at this point, the element of duality in this prophecy in regards to the city's invasion and destruction. It will happen again. Jesus' prophecy in Matthew twenty-four is clearly speaking about another attack on Jerusalem in the generation before He returns, and this correlates to Zechariah's prophecy (Zechariah 14:1,2).

Today the Jews have returned and are returning to the nation of Israel. They are currently awaiting a "prince that is to come," who they believe will be their long awaited messiah. But Daniel's prophecies do not reveal a benevolent deliverer, but quite the opposite. Another piece to the puzzle is added in Daniel's chapter eleven.

This chapter is in two parts. The first part from verses twenty-one through thirty-one describes the advent of

45

Antiochus Epiphanes, an evil ruler who was dedicated to destroying the Jew's religion. Antiochus was eventually defeated by the Maccabees which is foreshadowed in verses thirty-two through thirty-five of Daniel's prophecy. These verses serve as a bridge that transitions us to the picture of the final prince that is to come, the antichrist, (Daniel 11:36-45) of whom Antiochus is a foreshadow. We can see that this villain will be operating through the great tribulation of the latter days, also prophesied by Jesus which is known as the time of Jacob's trouble (Matthew 24:21, Daniel 12:1). In Daniel's prophecy we see that this time continues until the very end and all history cumulates at the last judgment at the feet of the Ancient of Days, God Himself.

Then we have to ask, where is the Jew's vision of them reigning from Jerusalem with their messiah in prophecy? When are those prophecies of a warless world fulfilled?

So far we have seen that the Messiah who was killed before the destruction of the second temple was Jesus, who prophesied that He would return as "lightning" (Matthew 24:27). It is here we need to examine Zechariah's prophecy which was deposited through his pen by the Lord to complete the picture of the vision of the future initiated through Daniel.

We see in verses one and two of Zechariah's chapter fourteen, that Israel is enduring yet another brutal captivity. This correlates to the time of Jacob's trouble which is the tribulation. This judgment was prophesied by Ezekiel. God would bring Israel's enemies upon them because of their sins (Ezekiel 38:16, 39:23), and this captivity would continue until the Lord's return as we are shown in Zechariah's prophecy.

We see in Zechariah that it is God who descends upon the Mount of Olives, the place from which Jesus also prophesied of this event in His Olivet discourse (Matthew 24:3).

When Jesus returns He destroys the world's oppressors including the antichrist and the beast of Revelation, (Rev. 13), which is the last world empire. He then begins His rule from Jerusalem (Rev. 19). We are told in the book of Revelation the Lord's reign is one thousand years. This time is far longer than a mere man can live.

Because Jesus is God manifest in human flesh (I Timothy 3:16), Jesus' reign of peace will last far longer than a man's average lifetime. This is one reason why Jesus had to come twice, once to be the last sacrifice for the sins of the people fulfilling all the foreshadows of the temple services and the prophecies in the Old Testament. After His resurrection from the dead He ascended and received His resurrected body which would enable Him to live forever and reign on earth for such a long time.

This same Jesus who is the image of God (Colossians 1:15) who dined with Abraham, (Genesis 18) will be the finale of all the Jew's expectations and they will finally be able to "Look upon Me (God the Father) whom they have pierced, and they shall mourn for Him (Jesus the Messiah) as one mourns for his only son" (Zechariah 12:10).

When all the prophecies concerning the messiah in the scriptures are taken into consideration, they only paint one portrait, no matter how many attempts are made to circumvent them. Jesus has to be the messiah because there is no other benevolent anointed one appearing anywhere in scripture after the destruction of the temple in 70AD. The antichrist, the evil prince that is to come is the false messiah that will deceive the Jews and all those who reject Jesus. One of the ancient Hebrew manuscripts describes this "prince that is to come" arriving upon "the wings of horrors."

The Jews will never reign from Jerusalem with their "messiah," except for possibly a brief interlude of deception before the antichrist demands to be worshipped in the place of God (II Thessalonians 2:3,4), the "abomination of desolation"

(Matthew 24:15, Daniel 9:27).

The repentant survivors of the time of Jacob's trouble, will be privileged to serve under the Anointed One that was killed, resurrected and supernaturally returns to be the true King as He always was and is, the Messiah Jesus.

The Jews' major objection to Jesus being the messiah is that He did not bring in the prophesied time of peace, a warless world. –

And He shall judge among the nations, and shall rebuke many people: and they shall beat their swords into plowshares, and their spears into pruning hooks; nation shall not lift up sword against nation, neither shall they learn war any more. – Isaiah 2:4.

As we have been shown from Daniel's prophecy, there is no warless world prophesied from the destruction of Jerusalem in 70AD to the judgment, a prophetic fact that the Hebrew scholars have obviously overlooked.

Let's go back and take another look at the time frame the angel gave Daniel for the advent of the messiah.

There were several commands issued by Persian kings to rebuild the temple and Jerusalem. The first one was issued by Cyrus to allow the Jews to return to their land and rebuild the temple (Ezra 1:1,2). The prophet Isaiah miraculously foretold this event approximately one hundred and fifty years earlier (Isaiah 45:1,13). The command to rebuild the city was given by King Artaxexes in 457 BC. (Nehemiah 2:18).

The seventy weeks are divided into three parts – seven weeks, sixty-two weeks and one week (verse 27).

The weeks are generally thought by most scholars to be "weeks of years." This interpretation is based on the year day theory taken from the examples in Ezekiel 4:6 and Numbers 14:34. Each day of the weeks in the prophecy represents a year, therefore each week represents seven years. So the time span illustrated in the prophecy looks like this. –

7 weeks = 49 years,
62 weeks = 434 years,
1 week = 7 years.

Seventy times seven equals 490, therefore the seventy week prophecy covers a time span of 490 years.

The seven weeks, which is designated as the time frame in which the temple is rebuilt, is distinguished in the prophecy from the sixty-two weeks, the longer period of time it took to rebuild the city, miraculously indicating the two distinct commands that were made, one to rebuild the temple by Cyrus and the command to build Jerusalem by Artaxexes.

When we compare the actual time it took to build the temple and Jerusalem, we understand that the time frames contained within the prophecy are symbolic.

The actual construction of the temple where forgiveness of sins would be resumed through animal sacrifice would only take from six to seven years. The rebuilding of the city took longer, it was completed in approximately seventy years. Therefore the construction of the temple and the city were completed well under the time frame of the seven weeks (49 years) to build the temple and sixty-two weeks, (434 years) to restore the city.

What we are being shown here is a prophetic designation of time that has been orchestrated to reveal the generation in history's calendar when thc Messiah was scheduled to arrive. This period of 483 years designates the amount of time required to "bring in everlasting righteousness" or the permanent removal of sin; something that animal sacrifice was never capable of doing. Remember, the entire prophecy is about this atonement (Daniel 9:24).

We were shown that - *after threescore and sixty-two weeks* (amount of years based on the solar calendar) *shall Messiah shall be cut off, but not for Himself: and the people of the prince that is to come shall destroy the city and the sanctuary; and the end shall be with a flood, and unto the end of the war desolations are determined (verse 26).*

So what we see here is that after the seven weeks, and the sixty-two weeks, (four hundred and eighty three years), the temple would again be destroyed which happened in 70 AD. And in the time period between the rebuilding of the temple and its destruction in 70 AD, the prophesied "anointed one," the Messiah would appear and be killed.

Using the solar calendar, when we add the four hundred and eighty-three years to the year four hundred and fifty seven BC, the year the decree was made by Artaxexes to rebuild the city, we are brought into the generation where Jesus made His grand entrance through the gates of Jerusalem riding on a donkey (Zechariah 9:9, Matthew 21:5). Therefore, the scriptures give us a remarkably accurate encapsulation of the time frame that chronicles the arrival of the prophesied Messiah.

Why would God use numbers that match the solar calendar to pin-point the Messiah's arrival, when the Jews used the lunar calendar which would place the end of the four hundred and thirty-four years arriving well after Jesus had come and gone?

God, through His foreknowledge, knew that the Jews would reject Jesus, but He would be received by the Gentiles as prophesied in the Scriptures. Knowing that the Gentiles use the solar calendar, God gave a time frame to Daniel that the Gentiles would decode, to encourage them that their faith in Messiah Jesus had not been misplaced, and they would recognize "the brightness of His rising" (Isaiah 60:3) - like the sun of the solar calendar!

God promised Abraham that he would be the father of many nations (Genesis 17:4) and a blessing to all the families of the earth (Genesis 12:3). God chose Abraham's lineage to birth redemption for the entire world through the Messiah Jesus.

Jesus has to be the Messiah.

A BIRD IN THE HAND

The fourteenth chapter of Leviticus, verses one through seven, is a wonderful example of the typology foreshadowing the Messiah that God has so brilliantly interwoven throughout the Holy Scriptures.

These particular verses in Leviticus describe a ritual for the cleansing of a leper. The priest commands that two birds be taken. One is killed in an earthen vessel over running water. Then a cedar stick with a scarlet cloth and hyssop are dipped in the blood of the bird, and so is the living bird. Then the priest sprinkles the leper with the blood on the cedar scarlet hyssop pole seven times and releases the living bird to freedom. Then the leper is pronounced clean.

I can picture a small child, the son of the priest, perhaps, watching this ceremony with a curious expression on his face. Afterwards, he asks his daddy; "Abba, what does it mean when you kill the bird and let the other go free?"

The priest doesn't really know what it means. He only knows that God has told them to do it that way. He might add in his explanation, that it is the blood that makes atonement for the soul and quote Leviticus 17:11. He doesn't know exactly why. It is the command of God and that is enough. He couldn't know what it all meant in his time, but now the scenario is quite a bit different.

A modern child has read these Scriptures and comes to his father, a pastor, perhaps. The child asks, "Daddy, what does this mean. Why is the one bird killed and the other goes free?"

The father smiles. He knows the answer because the shadows of the past have been unveiled in the light of prophecies fulfilled.

"The first bird is killed in an earthen vessel because

someday the Spirit of God would be in a man, the Messiah to save His creation. He would enter an earthen vessel and be killed and the water of His Holy Spirit would flow. The scarlet hyssop pole is symbolic of the cross He died upon in order to sprinkle His blood upon many nations, cleansing them from the leprosy of their sin. Then covered by the blood of the Messiah, the captive soul is set free and can rise into new eternal life because of the other's sacrifice. Do you understand?"

The child smiles. He understands and recites; "For God so loved the world that He gave His only begotten Son, that whoever believes in Him should not perish, but have everlasting life, because He was wounded for our transgressions and bruised for our sins." (*John 3:16, Isaiah 53:5*).

There is a flutter of wings outside the window and the child looks up in time to see a bird soaring out into the daylight, free.

THE MESSIAH JESUS AND ISAIAH 53

One of the pastors I met had a neighbor who was Jewish. This Jewish man vehemently rejected Jesus being the prophesied Messiah. One day while he was visiting the pastor, and they were having their usual theological discussion, the pastor opened his Bible and said, "I am going to read something from God's word. Tell me if it is from the Old Testament, or the new."

The pastor read him the fifty-third chapter from the book of Isaiah in the Old Testament. When he was finished, the Jewish man promptly exclaimed. "That's obvious. It's from the New Testament. It's all about Jesus." Then the pastor showed him that what he had read was actually from the Old Testament.

The pastor told me that the man's face turned as red as the carpet and he quickly fled the house.

It was sad that he could not remain to honestly and humbly admit that what he had been shown was an accurate prophetic declaration that Jesus was the promised Messiah, the Redeemer of mankind.

While Isaiah's prophecy is such an accurate description of the Messiah's suffering for the souls of mankind, the Jews for the most part are taught to believe that Isaiah is actually referring to the nation of Israel as mankind's redeemer. Because of the reference in verse eleven to God's righteous servant, and the fact that Israel is also called God's servant in other places in the Old Testament, the assumption is made without really consulting any other texts. But that was not always the case. The bulk of Jewish scholars recognized that the prophet Isaiah was writing about the Messiah. This correct interpretation is abundant in their writings and was the accepted interpretation.

In the Talmud (Sanhedrin 98b), it says, "The Rabbis said that Messiah's name is the Suffering Scholar of Rabbi's House (or 'Leper scholar'). For it is written 'Surely He has born our griefs and carried our sorrows yet we did esteem Him stricken, smitten of God and afflicted' (Isaiah 53:4).

In a commentary on Genesis, Rabbi Moses (the Preacher, 11th century), wrote; - From the beginning God has made a covenant with the Messiah and told Him, "My righteous Messiah, those who are entrusted to you, their sins will bring you into a heavy yoke'...And He answered, 'I gladly accept all these agonies in order that not one of Israel should be lost.' Immediately, the Messiah accepted all agonies with love, as it is written: 'He was oppressed and He was afflicted."

There are many other references to the suffering Messiah, but the traditional view began to change when it was noted that the Christians were using Isaiah 53 as an effective tool to bring Jews to the Messiah Jesus. The concept of the nation of Israel being the suffering servant of Isaiah's prophecy began to emerge from the shadows. Then a Rabbi named Rashi (1046-1105) promoted the budding concept that Isaiah was somehow speaking about the nation of Israel as the suffering servant. Many of the Rabbis of his day rejected Ravi's interpretation. One of them, Rabbi Moshe Kohen Ibn Crispin of Cordova, (1350), called it "forced and farfetched." He was absolutely right.

One of the Rabbis who refused to depart from the correct interpretation wisely noted; "Since Messiah bears our iniquities which produce the effect of His being bruised, it follows that whoso will not admit that the Messiah thus suffers for our iniquities, must endure and suffer for them himself." (Rabbi Elijah de Vidas (16th century) – Driver and Neubauer pg. 331).

I think that it's important to understand how the Jewish scholars choose to interpret scripture. They have a concept called "Takenot." This allows them to take a scripture out of context and build an entire doctrine around it. If all the other Rabbis are in agreement with it, then it becomes "law" even if it contradicts the Bible. So we can see why it is easy for them to ignore verse eight in Isaiah's prophecy that contradicts their interpretation that the nation of Israel is the suffering servant of Isaiah 53 and not Jesus.

In verse eight God makes a very definite designation between His people, Israel, and a specific individual, the Messiah: – "*...for the transgression of my* people (Isaiah's people, Israel) was **He** stricken."

It is also fairly ludicrous to believe that sinners can atone for the sins of another sinner, when all have sinned. Every human being is standing on the same feet of clay that fell in Eden's garden.

The pattern and means that God established for the remission of sins in the Old Testament, has also been removed or diminished. God stated very clearly that, *"The life of the flesh is in the blood, and I have given it upon the altar to make atonement for the soul, it is the blood that makes atonement for the soul."* – *Leviticus 17:11.* God has never changed or altered this requirement for the remission of sin, which is foreshadowed throughout the Old Testament.

When Jesus declared the Gospel to Nicodemus in John 3:16, He wasn't really stating anything new. The concept of grace, or having one's sins covered by sacrifice had already been established in the book of Genesis when God made the first sacrifice to cover Adam and Eve, showing us that their futile attempts to cover their own sin by self-effort was worthless and could never be accepted by God (Genesis 3:21). In view of this, to say that Israel could be the redeemer of mankind in Isaiah's prophecy, is ludicrous.

Jesus is the fulfillment of all the foreshadows, similitudes and typologies relating to the Messiah throughout the writings of Moses, the Psalms and the prophets. No else has ever, or will ever duplicate what the Messiah Jesus has fulfilled. Jesus is the prophesied Messiah

MATHEMATICAL ODDS

There are over three hundred prophecies concerning the Messiah interwoven throughout the Old Testament. Some of them are repetitions of the same prophecy. For example, the prophecy concerning Jesus being from the line of David is repeated about fourteen times. The number of non-repeating distinct prophecies is about one hundred and ninety.

M.B. Bleecker was an engineer who invented a helicopter prototype and the ram jet engine. He was also a Christian who took one hundred and fifty of the remarkable prophecies that Jesus fulfilled and calculated the odds of His fulfilling those prophecies. The odds of one man fulfilling one hundred and fifty prophecies in one lifetime are one in –

1,039,851,278,722,473,896,502,516,467,047,788,121,009,514,090,5 94,304.

The odds of Jesus fulfilling just eight of them in His lifetime are one in -

100, 000, 000,000,000,000.

God, The Ultimate Mathematician, has given us the numbers that point the way to the miracle of Jesus, the Messiah.

Prophecies Fulfilled by The Messiah Jesus

The first prophecy concerning the Messiah is found in Genesis 3:15.

And I will put enmity (hatred) *between you* (the devil) *and the woman* (Eve)*, and between your seed and her seed; it shall bruise your head, and you shall bruise His heel.*

The Messiah would be born through Eve's lineage, (Luke 3:38) and bruised by the devil. And the devil would be defeated by the Messiah.

Galatians 4:4, Revelation 12:5

Because the Messiah is to come through Abraham's lineage, his lineage is a blessing to all nations.-

And I will bless them that bless you, and curse him that curses you: and in you shall all the families of the earth be blessed (Genesis 12:3).
Seeing that Abraham shall surely become a great and mighty nation, and all nations of the earth shall be blessed in him (Genesis 18:18).

All the families of the earth are blessed because the Messiah would gather the Gentiles to God *(Isaiah 11:10, 42:6).*

The Messiah is a descendant of David. -

And there shall come forth a rod out of the stem of Jesse, (Matthew 1:6) and a Branch shall grow out of his roots (Isaiah 11:1). John 1:45, Acts 3:25. 13:22,23, Galatians 3:8

The Bible indicates the time of Messiah's coming. –

The scepter shall not depart from Judah, nor a lawgiver from between his feet, until Shiloh come; and unto Him shall the gathering of the people be (Genesis 49:10).

It was only under Roman rule, that the Jews were deprived of their ability to pass capital sentences. The "scepter" was removed and that is why the Jews had to bring Jesus to Pilate for sentencing. So we are told here the time in history when the Messiah would arrive.

The Messiah is to be born of a Virgin. –

Therefore the lord Himself shall give you a sign; behold, a virgin shall conceive, and bear a son, and shall call His name Immanuel (Isaiah 7:14). –

The name Immanuel means "God with us." In the original Hebrew the word used for virgin is almah, which means a young woman of marriageable age, which would mean a virgin in the Hebrew culture at that time. The same word, almah, is used to describe the virgin Rebekah in the Hebrew text of Genesis 24:43.

The New Testament Scriptures confirm Jesus' virgin birth. - Matthew 1:23, Luke 1:26,35, Luke 3:36

The Messiah, the sacrificial Lamb of God, would be born in Bethlehem; the very place where the lambs were raised for the temple sacrifices. –

But you, Bethlehem Ephratah, though you are little among the thousands of Judah, yet out of you shall He come forth unto Me that is to be ruler in Israel; whose goings forth have been from of old, from everlasting (Micah 5:2).

Matthew 2:1-6, Luke 2:4, John 7:42

The Messiah is descended from –
Shem - Genesis 9:27, Luke 3:36
Abraham – Genesis 12:3, 18:18, Matthew 1:1,2, Luke 3:34, Acts 3:25
Isaac - Genesis 17:19, 21:12, Matthew 1:2, Luke 3:34, Romans 9:7
Jacob – Genesis 28:14, Numbers 24:17, Matthew 1:2, Luke 3:34
Of the Tribe of Judah – Genesis 49:10, Micah 5:2, Matthew 1:2, Revelation 5:5
Of the house of David – Isaiah 9:7, Jeremiah 23:5, Matthew 1:1,6, Luke 3:31, John 7:42

Prophecies of Jesus' early life, ministry, death and resurrection. –

Children massacred as the result of His birth. – Jeremiah 31:15, Matthew 2:17,18

He would be called out of Egypt. - Hosea 11:1, Matthew 2:15

He would minister in Galilee. - Isaiah 9:1, 2, Matthew 4:15, 16

He would be a priest like Melchizedek. - Psalm 110:4, Hebrews 5:6, 6:20, 7: 17, 21

He would cleanse the temple. – Psalm 69:9, John 2:17

The anointing of God would be upon Him. – Isaiah 11:2, Psalm 45:2, Luke 4:18

He would enter Jerusalem on a donkey's colt. -Zechariah 9:9, Matthew 21:1-10, John 12:14-16

He would be betrayed. – Psalm 41:9, Matthew 26:15, Mark 14:10, 21

For thirty pieces of silver. – Zechariah 11:12, 13, Mathew 26:15, Mark 14:10, 21

He would be silent before His accusers. – Psalm 38:13, Isaiah 53:7, Matthew 26:63, 27: 12-14

He would suffer vicariously. - Isaiah 53:4-6, 12, Daniel 9:26, Matthew 8:17, Romans 4:25, I Corinthians 15:3, 4, Hebrews 9:28, I Peter 3:18

He would die with criminals. – Isaiah 53:9-12, Matthew 27:38, Luke 23: 39, 40

His hands and feet would be pierced. – Psalm 22:16, Zechariah 12:10, John 20:27

He would be insulted and mocked. - Psalm 109:25, 22:6,7, Matthew 27: 39, Mark 15:16-20,29

He would be scourged. – Psalm 129:3, Isaiah 53:5, Matthew 27:26

He would drink of vinegar and gall. – Psalm 69:21, Matthew 27: 34, 48, John 19:29

Lots would be cast for His clothing. – Psalm 22:18, Matthew 27:35, Mark 15:24, John 19:24

Like the Passover sacrificial lamb, not a bone of His would be broken. – Exodus 12:46, Psalm 34:20, John 19:36

He would be buried with the rich. – Isaiah 53:9, Matthew 27:57-60

He would rise from the dead. – Psalm 16:10, Matthew 27:63, 28:6, Acts 2:27-31 – and "see His seed" after death Isaiah 53:10.

He would ascend into heaven. – Psalm 68:18, 110:1, Luke 24:51, Acts 1:9, Ephesians 4:8-10, Hebrews 1:3

He would heal the blind. - David said in Psalm 146:8 that "The LORD (Yahweh) opens the eyes of the blind," yet there are no references in the Old Testament that record someone who is blind being healed. In the Messianic Prophecy of Isaiah 42:7 we are told that a characteristic of the Messiah would be that He would "open the blind eyes." Jesus inserted the phrase "recovering of sight to the blind" adapted from Isaiah 42:7 into His reading of Isaiah 61:1 which lists the Messiah's job descriptions that He applied to Himself. This incident is recorded in Luke 4:18. Jesus was sending a message to those who could discern, that opening the eyes of the blind was something that would identify Him as the Messiah.

Psalm 146:8 and the coordinating verses in Isaiah, are like arrows pointing through time to verify that Jesus is the prophesied Messiah, the only person in history to open the eyes of a man that was born blind (John 9:32).

There are also prophecies concerning the Messiah that have yet to be fulfilled. When we study Scripture it is important to understand that the entire counsel of God's Word must be consulted in order to understand it properly, or misinterpretations can arise. For example, there are prophecies that show us the Messiah is to be a suffering servant (Isaiah 53). At the same time we are shown that He will bring peace to the world (Isaiah 11). And the whole world will be in subjection to Him when He comes supernaturally a second time as recorded in Zechariah 14:4 and prophesied by Jesus (Matthew 24:27-30). So here we see that when all the Scriptures concerning the Messiah are taken into consideration, we understand that He first comes to give His life for the sins of mankind reconciling them to God, and that He will eventually come a second time, supernaturally as He has said, to bring peace to the earth under His rule.

SURELY I COME QUICKLY – JESUS
REVELATION 22:20

How to Receive the Gift of Eternal Life

For the wages of sin is death; but the gift of God is eternal life through Jesus Christ our Lord – Romans 6:23

At this moment you are a questioning child. God has placed the desire to know Him within your being and He is drawing you to Him. He begins by washing you with His Word, *for then faith comes by hearing, and hearing by the Word of God (Romans 10:17).* You must first understand and believe the beautiful Gospel of Jesus Christ.

The Word is near you, even in your mouth, and in your heart: that is, the Word of faith, which we preach; that if you shall confess with your mouth the Lord Jesus, and shall believe in your heart that God has raised Him from the dead, you shall be saved.

For with the heart man believes unto righteousness; and with the mouth confession is made unto salvation (Romans 10:8-10).

For God so loved the world, that He gave His only begotten Son, that whoever believes in Him should not perish, but have everlasting life.

For God did not send His Son into the world to condemn the world, but that the world, through Him might be saved (John 3:16, 17).

For the wages of sin is death, but the gift of God is eternal life through Jesus Christ, our Lord (Romans 6:23).

He was wounded for our transgressions; He was bruised for our iniquities: the chastisement of our peace was upon Him; and with His stripes we are healed (Isaiah 53:5).

For all have sinned and come short of the glory of God (Romans 3:23).

For when we were yet without strength, in due time Christ died for the ungodly (Romans 5:6).

Being justified freely by His grace through the redemption that is in Christ Jesus: whom God has set forth to be a propitiation through faith in His blood, (The Atonement) *to declare His righteousness for the remission of sins that are past, through the forbearance of God; to declare, I say at this time His righteousness: that He might be just and the justifier of him which believes in Jesus (Romans 3:24-26).*

Now that you have believed, you need to receive, that is repent. You must realize that you have sinned, confess your sins to the Lord and be willing to turn from them. This will initiate the beginning of God's sanctifying work to change you into the person He desires you to be. In this, God is no different than any good parent who wants the best for His children.

And the times of this ignorance God winked at; but now commands all men everywhere to repent (Acts 17:30).

The dictionary defines repentance as "Deep sorrow, compunction, or contrition for a past sin, wrong doing regret for any past action."

The Bible defines repentance as the need to change.

Therefore I will judge you, O house of Israel, everyone according to his ways, says the Lord God. Repent, and turn yourselves from all your transgressions; so iniquity shall not be your ruin (Ezekiel 18:30).

You seek the Lord while He may be found, you call upon Him while He is near. Let the wicked forsake his way, and the unrighteous man his thoughts: and let him return unto the Lord, and He will have mercy upon him; and to our God, for He will abundantly pardon (Isaiah 55:6, 7). See also Isaiah 59:20, Proverbs 28:13, Job 36:10.

Actually, it is sorrow for one's sins and the recognition that we need forgiveness that leads to repentance, the desire to change one's behavior. When we believe the gospel, that Jesus died for our sins, the acknowledgment that we have sinned which caused Jesus' suffering for us, should produce a deep remorse that results in repentance, a willingness to change, to turn from sins. Therefore repentance is the result of a genuine faith in the atonement.

...you sorrowed to repentance (II Corinthians 7:9).

For godly sorrow works repentance to salvation... (II Corinthians 7:10).

To you first God, having raised up His Son Jesus, sent Him to bless you, in turning away every one of you from his iniquities. (Acts 3:26).

I came not to call the righteous but sinners to repentance (Luke 5:32).

We are shown in John 15:5, that without Jesus "we can do nothing."

When we believe we receive the Holy Spirit, who then works with the believer to change us into the people God wants us to become. The process of becoming a "New Creature" (II Corinthians 5:17), is the result of salvation, not the means. The purpose of this transformation is to glorify God, validate the gospel message and bring others to Jesus.

In the first century church repentance, the need to turn from sin, was preached with the gospel.

They went out, and preached that men should repent (Mark 6:12).

And that repentance and remission of sins should be preached in His name among all nations, beginning at Jerusalem (Luke 24:47).

...to give repentance to Israel and forgiveness of sins (Acts 5:31).

...they should repent and turn to God, and do works meet for repentance (Acts 26:20).

You repent therefore, and be converted, that your sins may be blotted out (Acts 3:19).

Now begin your relationship with God through prayer. Make a formal invitation to receive Jesus into your heart and ask Him to forgive you of your sins. Through faith and repentance you are saved. Your sins are cleansed and the "Breath" of the Holy Spirit is received for the sanctification of your soul. Now are ready to begin your walk with God. –

Not by works of righteousness which we have done, but according to His mercy He saved us, by the washing of regeneration, and renewing of the Holy Spirit; which He shed on us abundantly through Jesus Christ our Saviour; that being justified by His grace, we should be made heirs according to the hope of eternal life (Titus 3:5-7).

But we are bound to give thanks always to God for you, brethren beloved of the Lord, because God has from the beginning chosen you to salvation through sanctification of the Spirit and belief of the truth (II Thessalonians 2:13).

Now that you have asked Jesus into your heart, you are ready to make a covenant with Him by water baptism. This is the "betrothal ceremony," the baptism into the Messiah, the commitment you make to walk with Jesus for the rest of your life as you await "The marriage supper of the Lamb" (Revelation 19:9).

We can be technically saved by faith without water baptism, as the believers in Acts 10:44-48, were saved and received the Holy Spirit before baptism, but we cannot receive the outcome of our faith, the salvation of our souls, without remaining in the faith (I Peter 1:9, Hebrews 3:14). This is the commitment that water baptism represents, and the commitment that God requires.

Water baptism is the fruit of a genuine repentance. When we are water baptized we are formally acknowledging our willingness to identify with Jesus' death and burial. When we rise up out of the water, we are symbolically leaving our old lives behind. We are making a commitment to God to become fully submerged in His Spirit and we cannot become the new creatures He desires us to be without this commitment. To the first century Christians and Apostles, water baptism was synonymous with receiving Jesus. Just as a genuine faith will produce fruit and a changed life, a genuine repentance will submit to this divinely appointed ordinance. A true believer does not need to be convinced he needs this commitment of water baptism, the Spirit compels him into the waters of obedience - and everywhere else the Holy Spirit leads him for the rest of his life.

The apostles baptized in the name of Jesus (Acts 2:38, 8:16,10:48,19:5,22:16). For that reason we should follow the apostolic example and baptize in the name of Jesus, which is the name (singular) of the Father, Son and Holy Spirit (Matthew 28:19); because Jesus is the fullness of the Godhead bodily (Colossians 2:9). God was in Christ reconciling the world to Himself (I Corinthians 5:19).

The Scriptures tell us that there are three dispensations of the Holy Spirit, the first is for sanctification (John 20:22). The second is the "Baptism of the Holy Spirit" or "full immersion" of the Spirit, which is for equipping. Here God bestows upon the believer gifts of His Spirit to help you in your walk with Him and to minister to others (Acts 2:1-4). The Spirit can also be received in subsequent dispensations for renewal to refresh and renew us in our walk with God when we need reinforcement (Acts 4:31).

Some believers receive the Baptism of the Holy Spirit upon initial belief, with others the Baptism of the Spirit can arrive at a later time. I believe that God intends the believer to receive the Baptism of the Holy Spirit with water baptism, but God's Spirit can arrive upon the believer before water baptism as the Scriptures indicate (Acts 10:44-48).

It is God's will and purpose for you to have His best and that includes all of His Spirit and subsequent gifting - *Quench not the Spirit (I Thessalonians 5:19).*

Jesus baptizes with the Holy Spirit (John 1:33) and He is the same yesterday, today and forever (Hebrews 13:8). There is no indication anywhere in the Scriptures that this aspect of Jesus' job description has ever been changed.

Continue to seek the Lord and ask Him for the gifts you will need to help you in your walk with Him. The gifts are always there for you because the *gifts and calling of God are without repentance (Romans 11:29),* which means they cannot be recalled, they are always available, even if they are not appropriated.

If you have had any involvement in the occult, do not seek the Baptism of the Spirit until you have been walking with the Lord for a long time and have had counselling from a qualified deliverance minister, as some gifts can be counterfeited by demonic entities. Mature believers have learned to "test" the spirits to discern legitimate manifestations of God's Spirit from counterfeits (I John 4:1).

The Holy Spirit will never lead you into sin, or tell you to do something that the Bible forbids. Saturate yourself in God's word.

My sheep hear My voice, and I know them and they follow Me(John 10:27).

My children, know this - you are loved, you are not forsaken and though the road of this life is difficult and exacting, you have the promise of something that is so much better. Do not neglect the offering of God's heart to yours.
You are loved.

Let not your heart
be troubled:
you believe in God, believe also in Me.
In My Father's house
are many mansions:
if it were not so, I would have told you.
I go to prepare a place for you.
And if I go and prepare a place for you,
I will come again,
and receive you to Myself;
that where I am, there you may be also.
I am the Way, the Truth, and the Life:
no one comes to the Father,
except by Me. – Jesus,
John 14:1-3,6

NOTES

MORE FROM THIS AUTHOR

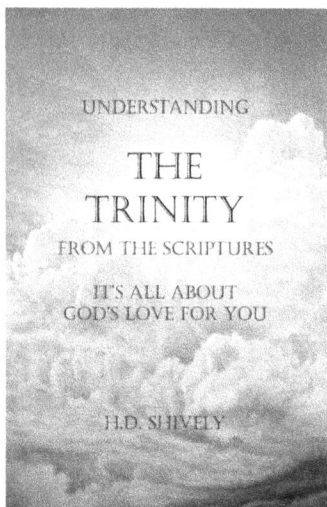

Understanding the Trinity from the Scriptures – It's all about God's Love for You Using the Scriptures as the sole source of this revelation, "Understanding the Trinity from the Scriptures" is a unique, easy to understand explanation of the unity of the Father, Son and Holy Spirit.

"If we cannot explain the Trinity from the Word of God, then we have no business teaching it as the Word of God." - H. D. Shively

ISBN-13: 978-1978167643

Holding onto Faith – Understanding the Book of Hebrews for You Today
The book of Hebrews was originally written to encourage Jewish believers in the Messiah Jesus to hold onto their faith, and not return to the old covenant, which God had fulfilled with the prophesied New Covenant. Holding onto Faith is an easy to understand expository study that effectively presents the basics of the Christian faith. "Holding onto Faith" is a relevant and vital resource for anyone who is seeking an effective tool for reinforcing the hope and uniqueness of what it means to be a believer in the Messiah Jesus.

ISBN 9781091760301

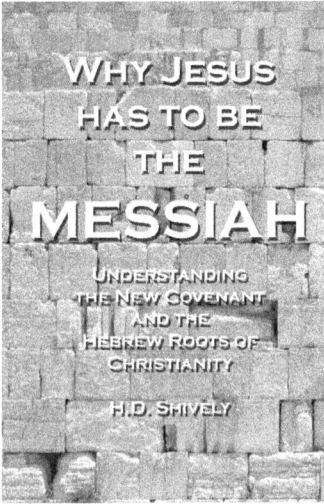

Why Jesus has to be the Messiah
Author and Bible scholar, H. D. Shively, directs us back through the centuries to explore the foreshadows and typologies that God has so brilliantly woven through His word to verify "Why Jesus has to be the Messiah."

You will be brought to an understanding of the unique plan of redemption for mankind that God has orchestrated from the beginning of creation.

You will understand how God and the Messiah are unified, and why it is not idolatry to worship God through Him.

You will be escorted through the writings of Moses and the prophets on a journey that leads to only one conclusion - Jesus is the prophesied Messiah.

ISBN 9798667887485

**Understanding the book of Revelation
– Hope for the times we are living now**
Revelation was written to encourage the Christian church in every generation. As recent history attests, the Euphrates River is drying, a significant event in Bible prophecy that is currently being fulfilled. As we continue on time's conveyor belt into the future, Revelation's message is as timely as today's newspaper.

Bible scholar, H. Deborah Shively, presents an easy to understand expository study that is designed to encourage and reinforce sincere believers in their faith. "Understanding the Book of Revelation" conveys a consistent theme of hope and victory in the face of the world's turmoil and instability. Yes, there is hope for the times we are living now.

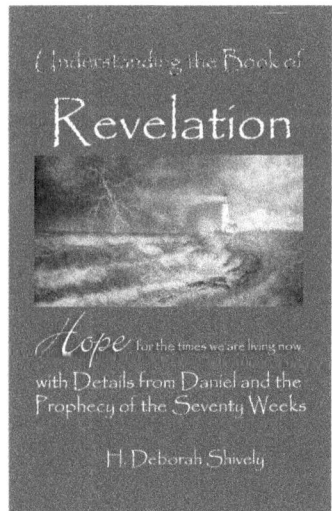

ISBN 9781985610699

www.ingramcontent.com/pod-product-compliance
Lightning Source LLC
Chambersburg PA
CBHW060702030426
42337CB00017B/2731